*«(...) Barcelona the beautiful and wise, where I left
so many things hanging on the altar of happiness that
now I mix from a little of the colour of the neck of
the dove of melancholy».*

Pablo Picasso, 12 January 1936

© Text: Claustre Rafart i Planas/Comercial Escudo de Oro, S. A.

© Photographs: Pablo Picasso, VEGAP, Barcelona, 1999.

© Edition: Editorial Escudo de Oro, S. A.

Rights of total or partial reproduction for photographs
and text reserved.

Design, lay-out and printing, entirely
created by the technical department
of EDITORIAL ESCUDO DE ORO, S.A.

I.S.B.N. 84-378-2147-9

Printed by FISA-ESCUDO DE ORO.

Legal Dep. B. 977-2006

PICASSO
in Barcelona

Claustre Rafart i Planas.

Editorial Escudo de Oro, S.A.

Barcelona at the turn of the century: the consolidation of modern Barcelona

Man sitting on beach.

The Ruiz Picasso family established its residence in Barcelona in the year 1895. The family settled in the Ciutat Vella district, or old city, the liveliest part of Barcelona which had been enclosed by medieval walls up to the year 1859. These walls were demolished as part of large-scale urban reforms affecting the immediate vicinity, expanding to affect nearby villages. The engineer Ildefons Cerdà drew up a project for reforming and extending the city, popularly known as the «Cerdà Plan». In it, he proposed the urbanisation of the entire Barcelona plain as far as the nearest villages, which were absorbed into the city, connected by an extensive gridwork of streets. In this way, the Eixample district of Barcelona came into being. The new constructions forming part of this massive undertaking illustrate the eclectic architectural language of the late-19th century, in which examples of the use of iron stand side-by-side with houses built from brick and stone and decorated with Neo-Gothic elements or undulating forms.

In the east of the city, this turn-of-the-century expansion also affected the old Ciutadella fortress, which had been demol-

False mountains of Montserrat in the Ciutadella Park.

ished some years previously and was now reformed, according to plans drawn up by the initial director of the work, Josep Fontserè, in preparation for the 1888 Universal Exhibition, the first to be held in Spain. The site was converted into a large park, the Parc de la Ciutadella, in which some of the 18th-century buildings were conserved, though put to new uses, and new ones built. Modern Barcelona was gradually taking shape.

By 1897, the project had absorbed the surrounding populations of Gràcia (joined to the city proper by Passeig de Gràcia, one of the prettiest boulevards in the entire city), Sants, Sant Andreu, Sant Martí, Les Corts and Sant Gervasi. Five years later, another key thoroughfare, Via Laietana, began to take shape as part of a reform project drawn up by Àngel Baixeras in 1880. The opening up of this street, forming a direct link between the Eixample district and the port, entailed the demolition of part of the old city centre and the restructuring of the urban fabric of the zone. Not far from here is the famous Rambla, one of the busiest thoroughfares in the city. At the end of this promenade, facing the sea, a monument to Christopher Columbus was erected, built by the architect Gaietà Buïgas in 1886. To the left of the Rambla is the Raval neighbourhood, one of the most densely-populated in the

5

city, whose lower reaches embrace Chinatown, the «Barri Xino», in those times the heart of low-life in Barcelona. One of the most important streets in the Raval neighbourhood is Carrer Nou de la Rambla which was known in those times as Conde del Asalto. This was where Picasso at one time had his studio. Nou de la Rambla leads into Avinguda Paral·lel, with its theatres, music-halls and night-clubs. Another important street, running parallel to this broad avenue is Carrer de Sant Pau, where the Romanesque Church of Sant Pau del Camp stands, a former Benedictine monastery which gives the street its name and which Picasso was to paint and draw.

Turn-of-the-century Barcelona stood out from all other Spanish cities. Flourishing industrial activity had created wealth and helped convert it into a European city. This was a «boomtown», full of opportunity, bursting with new ideas and political activity, as well as being home to serious social conflict. Taken together all in all, the good and the bad, Barcelona was a prosperous, cosmopolitan city. Picasso lived here during a decisive period, that of the formation of modern Barcelona. This was a

Corner of the cloister of Sant Pau del Camp.

Port.

The Barceloneta Beach.

«La Barceloneta».

Carrer de la Riera de Sant Joan, from the window of the artist's studio.

moment which saw the consolidation of an array of projects which transformed the entire structure of Barcelona, giving it a new image with the creation of an architectural legacy which, combined with its medieval and ancient heritage, make Barcelona an important artistic and culture centre.

Seascape. **Picasso in Barcelona**

Arrival. The first sojourn, 1895-1897

The Ruiz Picasso family arrived in Barcelona on 21 September 1895 from Málaga, from where they had departed on 13 September on board a small cargo boat, the *Cabo Roca*. After sailing up the Mediterranean coast of Spain, stopping off at the ports of Cartagena, Alicante and Valencia, their voyage ended in the city of Barcelona. During the voyage, Pablo produced a number of small paintings. Most of these are seascapes of subtle colour and warm luminosity, some of them clearly showing the influence of the seascapes of Emilio Ocón, painter and teacher at the San Telmo School of Arts and Crafts in Málaga, whom José greatly admired. No doubt, the young Pablo had seen works by this artist and other painters, friends of his father, during their summer visits to Málaga. It is interesting to note that the painting school of the Andalusian city enjoyed a period of enormous creativity in the second half of the 19th century, and the arrival in Málaga in the 1860s of painters Bernardo Ferrandis and

Antonio Muñoz Degrain, graduates of the Sant Carles Academy in Valencia, gave important impulse to the colourful, luminous art produced by the Málaga school.

Academic study.

Academic study.

The painter's family consisted of his parents, José Ruiz Blasco (1838-1913) and María Picasso López (1855-1939), and the two children, Pablo (1881-1973) and Lola (1884-1958). There was another daughter, Conchita (1887-1895) who caught diphtheria and died in Corunna (La Coruña). All were born in Málaga, where Picasso's father was a teacher at the San Telmo art school, curator of the City Museum, and painter. The move to Corunna was forced by economic reasons. Don José obtained a teaching post which had become vacant at the Guarda Art School. The tragic loss of little Conchita only increased the gloom and unhappiness of the father, who never got used to the Atlantic climate of the Galician capital.

In the spring of 1895, Professor Román Navarro García, of the Llotja de Barcelona Art Academy, offered Picasso's father a post. Accepting the offer, Don José went to the Catalan capital to take up his new post as professor of «figure drawing».

Academic study.

Female nude, back.

Pablo Picasso was nearly fourteen years old when he arrived in Barcelona. He was a young adolescent whose education and family background had immersed him in the environment of official art. In order to continue and consolidate his official studies, which he had begun in Corunna in the 1892-1893 academic year, Pablo enrolled at the Llotja de Barcelona Art School. Moreover, his father, Don José, also kept a close eye on the budding young artist's development and training. It is important to remember that Picasso's artistic beginnings, during his childhood and youth, were marked by strict discipline based on drilling in the most conventional of artistic canons, a traditional education which helped him to attain a solid grounding in his trade.

Despite this, Picasso breathed in the bracing airs of Modernism from the very streets of the city and, though to young to play an active part in the movement, realised that there was another world of art and culture besides the academic.

Picasso made his first Catalan friends at La Llotja Art School: Manuel Pallarès (1876-1974), a young aspiring artist from

11

Portrait of the artist's mother.

Horta de Sant Joan, with whom he maintained a close friendship until the end of his life, Joaquim Bas, the sculptor Josep Cardona, Bernareggi a painter of Argentinian origins...

A constant of Picasso's work during his formative years is his simultaneous cultivation of two tendencies, academic and free art forms. The academic branch is found in his art school exercises, basically copies of plaster models, followed by copies from real-life and from museum works by various artists. His freer, more intuitive work is concentrated, principally, on two genres, the landscape and the portrait, themes he cultivated throughout his life, though the landscape only intermittently. The exercise of both genres, in those times, helped him gain entrance into the world of official art.

As in Corunna, the main subjects of his portraits are his family: his mother, his sister, Lola and, above all, his father, a crucial figure for the young man throughout his formative period. He also carried out a series of self-portraits.

Portrait of the artist's father.

Self-portrait.

Landscape is a predominant genre throughout the periods of Picasso's artistic formation, and are an essential, constant exercise. The first landscapes, apart from one or two painted in Málaga, were produced in Corunna. In Barcelona, Picasso constantly explored his environment, and his work portrays many of the features of his new surroundings: the sea, the beach in the Barceloneta district, the Ciutadella Park...

In summer, in Málaga, the landscape is the inspiration behind his painting, with the exception of the **Portrait of Aunt Pepa**, one of the key portraits in this formative period and a clear illustration of the young artist's concern to capture the human essence. Picasso also completed an extraordinary documentary report on his environment, the mountains of Málaga, whose epicentre is **Mountain Landscape**, painted with a freer brushstroke, lively colour and great luminosity. He continued using the tonal qualities he had begun to employ before leaving Barcelona, not dissimilar from the painting of a group of artists known as the Colla del Safrà («The Saffron Group»), whose members included Nonell, Mir, Pichot, Gual, etc. One of the key features of the work of this group was a lively use of colour. Picasso saw their works at an exhibition

13

Landscape.

Portrait of Aunt Pepa.

*The First
Communion.*

to which he contributed **The First Communion**. These landscapes, along with the last ones he completed in Barcelona, show Picasso beginning to distance himself from academic art, falteringly at first, as he was still very young and had not yet acquired the basis necessary to consolidate this rupture.

Religious and historic subject-matter are important themes in official artistic circles, and it is no surprise, therefore, that Picasso should work on them intensively over the years 1896 and 1897. He chose a religious theme for his debut in the Barcelona art world, **The First Communion**, which he presented at the Third Fine Art and Artistic Industry Exhibition.

This is a large oil painting featuring a classical composition and which shows the influence of a work entitled **Figure** by Professor José Garnelo Alda (1866-1944), who allowed Picasso to work in his studio in Plaça Universitat. The following year, Picasso once again presented a work at an official exhibition, the National Art Exhibition in Madrid. This was the large oil **Science and Charity**, which has a forerunner in **The Patient**, painted in Corunna in 1894. Picasso was strongly influenced by Enrique Paternina's **Visit to his Mother**, which he had seen at the previous year's exhibition, and by **Visit to the Doctor**, by the painter Martínez de la Vega. Now, Picasso's father hired the young artist a studio in Carrer de la Plata to allow him to work. The oil, preceded by various preparatory sketches, highly naturalistic and in full accordance with contemporary taste at the turn of the century, features two highly fashionable themes: philanthropy and increasing interest in the advances of science, personified in the nun and the doctor –Picasso's father– respectively.

Science and Charity.

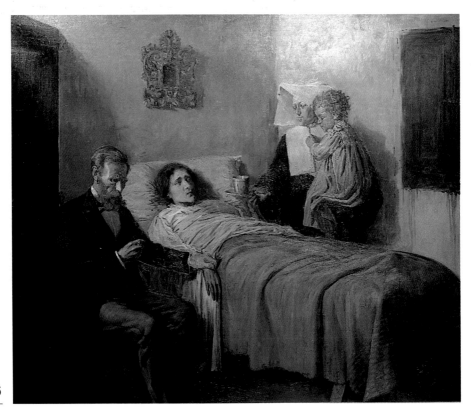

«Salón del Prado».

A brief parenthesis: Madrid and Horta de Sant Joan, October 1897-January 1899

Picasso's family saw the young Pablo as a promising offi-cial artist, and for this reason considered it essential that he should consolidate his academic training at the San Fernando Art School in Madrid, the most prestigious at that time.

This was the first time Picasso had left the family environ-ment, in a sojourn lasting from October 1897 to June 1898. However, a letter to his friend Joaquim Bas in Barcelona, dated 3 November 1897, testifies to the fact that he soon rebelled against the educational system at San Fernando. In the letter, he describes his complete rejection of acade-mic teaching methods, which he considers obsolete, and praises the work, principally, of Velázquez, followed by El Greco, Teniers, Titian and Rembrandt, amongst others. Practically no trace has survived of his time at the school, but there are many drawings and a few paintings which reaffirm his desire to distance himself from the teachings he

17

Copy of a portrait of Felipe IV, painted by Velázquez in 1652-1653.

received in his classes and his growing interest for land-scape and the great masters whose paintings he admired at the Prado Museum, where he made copies of works by Velázquez and Goya, as well as of bullfighting scenes.

Nooks and corners, such as the **Salón del Prado** and **El Retiro Lake**, form the chronicle in art which Picasso left of the city at the end of the 19th century, featuring his por-trayals of classical personalities of popular, «castizo» Madrid. It was in Madrid, too, that he met up again with Bernareggi, his former fellow pupil at La Llotja art school. Bernareggi and the Catalan artist Eusebi Güell were his companions in his escapades in the Spanish capital.

When Picasso stopped going to class, his family refused to go on subsidising him, though his father sent him what

Various sketches of women with shawls.

Cart-driver.

money he could. In June, Pablo caught scarlet fever, returning to Barcelona once over the worst of it. Of his brief visit we have a series of works of a social nature, featuring street-scenes and everyday events depicted in a markedly *fin-de-siècle* artistic language. Soon, he left for Horta de Sant Joan (in those days known as Horta d'Ebre) in the Terra Alta county of Tarragona, to stay with his friend Pallarès in a visit lasting from the end of June 1898 to January 1899, after which he returned once more to Barcelona.

Picasso adapted to his new surroundings in no time, rejoicing in nature and sharing the life of the countrypeople. His sojourn in Horta de Sant Joan was so important to his life that years later he confessed to Sabartés, his friend and first biographer that «Everything I know, I learnt in Pallarès's village».

The paintings and drawings Picasso did in Horta de Sant Joan are extraordinarily attractive due to their naturalism. These are works informed by the direct nature of their execution, spontaneous, full of light... Their iconography forms a magnificent graphic report on rural life in all its aspects:

19

El mas del Quiquet.

Mountain landscape.

Boy and other sketches.

the surrounding landscape, country people, animals... All full of life and authenticity, as we can see in the oil paintings **Mountain Landscape** and **El mas del Quiquet** and the drawing **Child** and other sketches. From the stylistic point of view, these works represent the final break with strict academic rules and a hymn to freedom of artistic expression.

The brief period of time embracing Picasso's first important visits to Madrid and Horta de Sant Joan formed the starting-point of his incursion into avant-garde currents. When he returned to Barcelona in January 1899, the young artist had already achieved enormous freedom of line and artistic expression.

Rooftops and Santa Marta church.

The return: immersion in the Catalan artistic avant-garde, 1899-1900

Back in Barcelona, the artist, full of new life, took on with relish the challenge of a new century which began with the euphoria of the Modernist postulates, which had dominated art since the closing decade of the 19th century. More receptive than ever to his surroundings and free of the yoke of official art, this was the perfect moment to become a fully-fledged member of the Catalan artistic avant-garde, which he made contact at the Els Quatre Gats café, artistic and cultural headquarters of Modernist Barcelona.

Though fast becoming a virtuoso, Picasso returned to his drawing classes, attending those of the Cercle Artístic de Barcelona. This pleased his father, who had still not lost the hope of seeing young Pablo triumph as a salon painter. The drawings he produced at the Cercle Artístic were real-life copies of models nude and clothed, above all female nudes, in which one can observe how he gradually forsakes detail for form. His outlines are more lightly-sketched, ductile and voluble, he scarcely takes time to

«La chata».

Female nude, profile.

add tone to his work, concentrating on shading certain zones with a few light strokes, more or less modulated. Some of these drawings feature notably sharp contours.

Whilst he worked on these exercises, he also continued to portray his family, above all his father, his preferred model between 1895 and 1899. Picasso also continued to produce both realistic representations and caricatures of social and popular themes. The night-spots and denizens of Barcelona's low-life areas are the protagonists of such outstanding works as **The Couch**. Street-scenes, sea-side «merenderos» (snack bars), nooks and crannies in the historic city centre or the roofs of old Barcelona populate an urban chronicle of this turn-of-the-century period: **The roofs of the Church of Santa Marta from the studio in Riera de Sant Joan, Carrer de la Riera de Sant Joan seen from the artist's studio**... In the city streets, Picasso found picturesque characters, alone or in groups, who captured the

23

*Couple in an
Andalusian patio.*

*Lola, the artist's
sister.*

Portrait of an unknown man after El Greco.

attention of the young artist in his avid exploration. Such was young Pablo's expressive urge that at times he feverishly began a new drawing before completing the one in hand.

Over the first few months of 1899, Picasso became a fully-fledged member of the circles which met at Els Quatre Gats «beerhouse-tavern-hostel». The name, Catalan for «The Four Cats», also signifies a small quantity of something, that is to say, when a group is very small, we say they are «quatre gats». Els Quatre Gats was a beerhouse modelled on Rodolphe Salis's Le Chat Noir in Paris. It had a small theatre, for shadow theatre, puppet shows, cabaret, etc, and exhibition rooms. The locale opened to the public on 12 June 1897, thanks to the efforts of Miquel Utrillo and with the co-operation of painters Rusiñol and Casas, amongst others. The manager was Pere Romeu, a most singular character. The situation, on the ground floor of the Casa Martí in Carrer de Montsió, was ideal, this being a Modernist building designed by the architect Puig i Cadafalch, closely-linked to intellectu-

al and political Modernism. Contemporary critic Raimon Casellas defined the house as a «mixture of archaeology and Modernism, of love of the ancient and passion for the new». Until its closure in the summer of 1903, Els Quatre Gats was the centre of artistic and intellectual debate in Barcelona, though it began to lose its pre-eminence after 1901.

The venue combined artistic, literary and musical events and activities, as well as publishing an illustrated periodical. Its debates attracted the cream of the Modernists and Post-Modernists who made up Catalan avant-garde circles, with their constant curiosity and spirit of innovation and renewal. This, then, was the ambience in which the young artist from Málaga began to move, one where, as well as conversing, artists, even the youngest, could display their works in collective and

The divan.

Woman with shawl, seated.

individual exhibitions organised on an informal basis. Picasso's fellow-members in this avant-garde cultural society included: Carles Casagemas, Jaume Sabartés, Ramon and Cinto Reventós, Àngel and Mateo Fernández de Soto...

Picasso found enormous stimulation in the Modernists, and it was through them that he learned about artistic and literary tendencies in the rest of Europe, imported by Catalan painters like Casas and Rusiñol, amongst others, who came and went between Barcelona and Paris and who gave him new points of reference, opened up new horizons to him. These new perspectives are reflected in the works he produced during that period, during which he also played an active part in different activities in the city, working generously on a variety of initiatives. It was during this period that

27

The violinist in the street.

28

The kiss.

Portrait of Jaume Sabartés, seated.

Joan Vidal Ventosa.

he began to develop his talent as an illustrator, a field which he would later cultivate extensively. December 1899 also saw his beginnings as a poster artist, a new and important field of graphic expression in the late-19th century. In Catalonia, both the graphic industry and poster art became firmly established during the Modernist period, and Picasso was encouraged to develop his own skills by the attraction of a new medium and the incentives of the prizes offered.

In February 1900, Picasso staged a one-man exhibition in the Sala Gran of Els Quatre Gats. This show, a rebuttal of Ramon Casas, official portrait artist to the Catalan bourgeoisie at the time, and factotum at the beerhouse, was what really opened up the inner circles of the Modernist movement to the young Picasso. Most of the works in the exhibition are drawings, portraits of his friends in charcoal or mixed media, using new tonalities and an abundance of pastel, a medium in which he was to continue working over the following months. This was

29

the high point of Picasso's involvement with Barcelona culture. He staged another exhibition in June that same year.

Portrait-caricature of Rocarol.

Bullfighting scenes are a constant in his work, and between 1899 and 1900, the theme of tauromachy comes up time and again in his oils and drawings, making this the most important period of Picasso's formative years in terms of his use of bullfighting iconography. The concern with tauromachy had much to do with the atmosphere of the Barcelona of the period, for in June 1900 Las Arenas Bullring was opened, eclipsing the venue which already existed in the Barceloneta district. As Sabartés puts it: «... others went with him to the bullfighting on days when there was a *corrida*; to the café every afternoon and evening; to the Edèn Concert and the taverns of El Paralelo, or to other places their carefree youth led them to frequent».

Portrait of Santiago Rusiñol.

Picasso's links with Els Quatre Gats continued, though gradually losing intensity, right up to the closure of the establishment on 26 June 1903. Nevertheless, the period when he was most closely involved with its activities was a very short one, from around January 1899 to September 1900, a year and a half or so which coincided with the most brilliant moment in the café's history. It was here that Picasso became convinced of the need to go to Paris, the aim of so many artists at that time.

Menu in Els Quatre Gats and Caricature of Pere Romeu as a Boer, and other sketches.

Self-portrait.

Picador with «monosabio».

The spirit of the Barcelona avant-garde in Picasso's work in Paris and Madrid in 1900 and 1901

In the dressing-room.

Paris, then, had become a kind of Mecca to the artists of the younger generation of Modernists, amongst whom Picasso was the most outstanding talent and group leader. Jaume Sabartés again: «There is Paris. There is Europe, and Picasso still has not crossed the Pyrenees. We breathed an atmosphere infested with Northern modernisms. The only thing important is the imported: the fashion of Paris».

The Universal Exhibition in Paris, which marked the beginning of the new century, generated considerable stimulus for the artists of the time, above all for Picasso, one of whose works was selected to form part of an exhibition. He went to Paris with his friend, the painter Carles Casagemas.

The embrace. ▷

The correspondence the two young artists maintained with their friends in Barcelona, as well as various of Picasso's works of the time, show their close ties with regulars at the beerhouse in Carrer de Montsió who were now in the French capital: Ramon Pichot, Peius Gener, Alexandre Riera, Isidre Nonell... It was, as one author put it, as if the spirit of Els Quatre Gats had journeyed to Paris for the Universal Exhibition.

Picasso's production over these months, some of them caricatures, show clearly the mixture of the influences which he brought with him from Barcelona with those he discovered in Paris. His line is more mature now, giving his drawings increased freshness and spontaneity. Paris opened up new horizons to the young artist, and these new perspectives soon found their place in his creative work.

The pair returned to Barcelona at Christmas, en route to Málaga, where they saw in the New Year. On 28 January, Picasso went to Madrid, where he stayed until June 1901. But the spirit of Els Quatre Gats accompanied the artist on his second important sojourn in the Spanish capital. Madrid, at that time the centre of official painting, opened up encouraging perspectives to him for projecting the new avant-garde currents he had become familiar with in Barcelona and Paris. In Madrid, too, he met up again with a fellow pupil at La Llotja art school, Francesc d'Assís Soler, with whom he created the magazine *Arte Joven*.

«La diseuse».

The two young men hoped to bring together the most progressive and inquisitive figures from the world of art and literature around their magazine, and to generate an ambience similar to that which was created around the Barcelona magazine *Pèl & Ploma,* whose artistic director was Ramon Casas, whilst literary aspects were in the hands of Miquel Utrillo. In the Madrid publication, Picasso and Soler divided these tasks in the same way, the former dealing with art, the latter with literature. Close links were forged between the two magazines with an eye to establishing ties between the most advanced artistic and literary circles in the two cities. *Arte Joven* is the testimony of two young men eager to regenerate the world, a desire they shared with a group of young people who were to form the so-called «Generation of 98» some of whose members contributed to the publication.

The Wait (Margot). Picasso returned to Barcelona on his way back to Paris, his presence made necessary by forthcoming exhibitions. At the first of these, Miquel Utrillo organised a joint show with Ramon Casas at the Sala Parés, a gallery which had become a key point in the Barcelona art world. At the second, Picasso's first dealer, Pere Mañach, a Catalan established in Paris, organised his first exhibition in the French capital, jointly with Basque painter Iturrino at the Vollard Gallery.

La Nana.

Still-life. Picasso then returned to Paris, remaining in the French capital from June 1901 to January 1902. This period was marked by an intensified search for new subjects and new forms of expression, in independence and the desire to follow his own impulses. Low-life and the night-life of the city which exercised such a powerful attraction on him in Barcelona continued to be an important theme in his work over his early months in Paris, where he was seduced by the pleasures of La Belle Époque. The influence of Toulouse-Lautrec is evident in various drawings with their elegant lines and arabesque, such as **The end of the number** and **La diseuse**. He also produced paintings with an expressionism reminiscent of the work of Steinlen, such as in **The Embrace**. In **Margot** or **The Wait** and **La Nana**, he displays enormous energy and originality due, to a large extent, to his light, freely-flowing brushstroke, which Lafuente Ferrari called «macrodivisionism» and which imbued the work with a mosaic-like texture. The strident colourist style of these works, another key element in this period, have led to them being considered pre-Fauvist in style.

37

Blue portrait of Sabartés.

The Blue Period 1901-1904

Picasso's artistic career was not long in producing a first personal style, one known as his Blue Period.

The northern airs –Schopenhauer, Nietzsche, Wagner, etc– which impregnated the artistic and literary world of Modernist Barcelona more than ever informed his work now, enriched by the atmosphere and feeling found in the texts of such French symbolist writers as Rimbaud, Baudelaire and, above all, Verlaine, whose work Picasso was now reading thanks to the urging of his friend, the Jewish poet Max Jacob. Picasso's work at this time also reveals the influence of French symbolist painters like Maurice Denis and, above all, Puvis de Chavannes, and Expressionists such as the Norwegian artist Edvard Munch.

Roofs of Barcelona.

Woman, seated.

His work gradually underwent a substantial thematic and chromatic change. The mundane world he used to chronicle with such chromatic exuberance disappears little by little and a new, more symbolic world emerges. This world is peopled by characters mostly from the margins of society. The social problems of contemporary Barcelona concerned many artists (Casas, Nonell, Mir...) who did not hesitate to portray in their works the crude reality the saw in the impoverished outlying districts of the city.

Picasso set off along the path to his new blue universe with a series of works commemorating his friend Casagemas, who had committed suicide on 17 February in the Café de l'Hippodrome in Paris. Between late-autumn 1901 and the end of January 1902, the colour blue impregnates the compositional space of

his works. Moreover, his figures become more and more deformed, as in **Woman in a Bonnet**. These are works full of feeling and with a strong spiritual component, for Picasso was convinced that art emanates from sadness and suffering. This radical change in his work, one which was to become general throughout his production over the coming years, was brought about by series of personal, environmental, cultural and even social factors.

Women, men, mothers and children, entire families..., hungry, huddling together, scarcely able to support their own weight, blind, mad, vulnerable... these are the protagonists of much of Picasso's work from 1901 to 1904, when he divided his time between Paris and Barcelona. These works include **Defenceless** and **Woman with a**

Defenceless.

lock of hair. People, individually or in groups, with no present or future, portrayed by the artist not in denouncement, but simply as mute testimonies to a reality he perceived around him. Their great eyes do not shine, their gaze is lost in the horizon, desperate. Their stretched, elongated bodies and extremities, as in **The Madman**, are the reflection of a mannerist Expressionism Picasso inherited from El Greco, painter from the Spanish «Siglo de Oro», as he himself told Brassaï: «(...) If the figures in the Blue Period are elongated, it is probably due to his influence (...)».

The landscape now reappears in certain drawings and oils though, in many cases, at the service of personages, as in **Mother and son by the sea**. These are generally bucolic, impersonal landscapes with clearly symbolist influence.

The madman.

Recumbent nude, with Picasso seated at his feet.

The sea, a favourite theme during Picasso's formative years, now returns thanks to the suggestive power of its green and blue tones and its sheer enormity, two features generating a sensation of mystery and melancholy perfectly adapted to what the artist sought to express. The urban landscapes, featuring Picasso's immediate surroundings, are also imbued with this strongly subjective art. From his studios, Picasso painted the rooftops of the city illuminated by a crepuscular light, as in **Roofs of Barcelona**.

The brothers Mateu and Àngel Fernández de Soto, with Anita.

The new style did not prevent his friends and companions in the artistic events at Els Quatre Gats from continuing to be featured in some of his works. Sabartés, Àngel Fernández de Soto, Sebastià Junyer... are portrayed and imbued with the colour inspired by such poets as Novalis, whose work could be read in the magazines of Barcelona at the turn of the century thanks to the excellent Catalan translations by the poet Joan Maragall.

At the same time, Picasso continued to produce humorous works and caricatures, at times sarcastic and burlesque in style. These are ironic portraits of friends and acquaintances, as well as self-portraits, precise, spontaneous entertainments, characters described, generally, in a synthetic manner with a quick, light stroke.

43

Series of five drawings (numbers 1, 2, 3, 4 and 6) for an «auca», comic strip, of six on the theme of Picasso's fourth trip to Paris, in the company of Sebastià Junyer.

Goodbye to Barcelona, April 1904

Picasso's artistic evolution was by now such that it could only be a matter of time before he left Barcelona. For months now, he had worked little and had shown signs of becoming jaded. It was becoming more and more obvious that he needed a change, something which would give him new inspiration. Picasso himself was aware of this, as were his friends. Carles Junyer, in a long article full of praise for the artist published in *El Liberal* on 24 March 1904, makes this clear. The piece proclaims that Picasso's work cannot be compared with that of any other artist in the country, it is something else, and that he will soon return to Paris. That same day, Miquel Sarmiento published an article in *La Tribuna* in which he affirms that Picasso misses the «fever» of the French capital and that he feels he is just passing through Barcelona.

Shortly after this, on 12 April, Picasso set off on his last, definitive journey to Paris. He was accompanied by his unconditional friend and supporter Sebastià Junyer Vidal. The two young men were full of great plans and high expectations before an uncertain future, eager to blaze a trail to the Mecca of art at the time. The journey is commemorated by a humorous «auca», or comic strip narrating the adventures the pair met along the way.

Picasso had left Barcelona behind him for good, and now installed himself in Paris, in the working-class district of Montmartre. The new surroundings, new friends and a suit-

able environment formed a stimulus pressing the young artist on to seek new forms of plastic expression. His work gradually incorporates new subjects, most of them personages from the circus and cabaret, whilst tender fawns and pinks gradually replace his earlier colours, dominating the artist's new cosmos. This is the Rose Period, during which Picasso painted markedly classical-style oil **Portrait of Mrs Canals**, featuring the lovely Roman lady Benedetta Bianco, wife of Picasso's artist friend Ricard Canals. In this work, Picasso takes Benedetta out and isolates her from the folkloric context of the box in the bullring where Canals painted her beside Picasso's mistress, Fernande Olivier.

Picasso searched and explored right to the end of his life, in Paris and elsewhere in France. He never resigned himself to becoming trapped by a single style or artistic language, even if he himself had created them. His life was one of constant evolution, and his artistic development can best be defined as a process of constant renewal.

Visits to Barcelona

In the summer of 1906, Picasso returned to Barcelona in the company of Fernande Olivier. They were one their way to Gósol, a village in the Berguedà county (Barcelona province). During their stay in the city they met up with old friends and visited the places they used to frequent. The young people, accompanied by Ramon Reventós, visited Joan Vidal Ventosa's studio, known as El Guayaba, in Plaça

Portrait of Mrs Canals.

Harlequin.

de l'Oli. A photograph immortalising them has become the direct testimony of their visit to Barcelona. Shortly before Picasso's arrival, in May, Joan Maragall, the great Catalan poet, had published his book *Enllà*, from which Picasso took a poem, *Vistes al mar*, copying it out and translating it into French in his sketchbook, known as the **Carnet català**.

At this time, Picasso was leaving the Rose Period behind him and seeking a new language of plastic expression. The experience he brought with him from Paris, along with that gained during his stay in Gósol, a village of wild landscapes lying in the heart of the Southern Pre-Pyrenees in a valley at the foot of Mount Pedraforca, combined to inspire him to embark on a work of schematisation, volumetrisation and

47

Woman with shawl.

simplication of forms. He continued this work in Paris, and the process eventually took the form of the oil painting **Les demoiselles d'Avignon** (1907), an artistic breakthrough which signified the first shot in the revolutionary process leading to the creation of Cubism.

When Picasso and Fernande returned to Barcelona, in 1909, on their way to Horta de Sant Joan, the artist was fully immersed in this new art form, which revolutionised the concept of traditional art. Picasso painted a portrait of his friend Manuel Pallarès in his studio over the apartment at 54, Carrer Pelai, and also visited El Guayaba, which had moved to 17 Carrer de la Riera de Sant Joan, in his old studio.

Male, seated.

It was during this trip to Barcelona that Picasso also took up the magazine *Arte Joven*, which he had set up in Madrid with Francesc d'Assís Soler, once more. The idea was not a great success, however, and only one issue came out, dated 1 September 1909.

The following year, at the end of June, Picasso visited Barcelona once more, accompanied by Fernande and their friends the painter André Derain and his wife. From the Catalan capital, they went on to Cadaqués at the invitation of their friend the painter Pichot and his companion, Germaine.

On 3 June 1913, Picasso's father, Don José, died. At the

time, Picasso was in Ceret with his mistress, Eva (Marcelle Humbert), from where the artist came to Barcelona for the funeral.

Five years later, in 1917, Picasso visited Barcelona twice, firstly, for a short sojourn in January, when he spent a few days with his family. This was probably from 16 January to 1 February, when he returned to Paris. The second visit was a longer one, lasting from June to November. The avant-garde art movement was at that time becoming consolidated around the Dalmau Galleries, which had staged exhibitions by such artists as Torres García, Duchamp, Gleizes, Léger... and Picasso himself.

The young artist then collaborated with the Ballets Russes, the ballet company directed by Serge Diaghilev. The troupe lodged at the Pension Ranzini at 22, Passeig de Colom, whilst Picasso stayed at his family's home in Carrer de la Mercè. He had fallen in love with the dancer Olga Kokhlova (1891-1955), whom he married the following year.

During the Spanish tour, the company performed from 23 to 30 June and from 5 to 12 November at the Gran Teatre del Liceu. On Saturday 10 November, they presented the ballet *Parade*, the only production in which Picasso took part.

Over these months, the artist became immersed once more in the Barcelona art and social scene, re-encountering many of his old friends from Els Quatre Gats: Ramon Casas, Miquel Utrillo, Àngel Fernández de Soto, the Reventós brothers... Two events were organised in his honour. The first was a banquet-homage in honour of the painters Iturrino, Maeztu and Picasso at the Laietanes Galleries in June, according to the graphic testimony published in the local magazine *Vell i Nou*, which also dedicated articles to Picasso, as well as publishing some of his drawings. The second took place on 12 July at the Lyon d'Or, one of the most prestigious restaurants in the city.

Picasso's sojourn in the city at this time produced a series of works illustrating the range of styles in which he was working. Here, side-by-side with the late Cubism of

Passeig de Colom.

Blanquita Suárez or **El Passeig de Colom**, we find the precise pointillism of **La Salchichona**, the markedly Expressionist **Horse being gored** and a return to the classical Mediterranean source of inspiration in **Harlequin** These are the last works Picasso produced in Barcelona.

After 1917, there is certain evidence of only three more visits by Picasso to the city of Barcelona. One took place in October 1926, a second in mid-August 1933, and the last the following year during a trip to Spain. It was during this last stay in Barcelona that Picasso visited, before its official opening, the room devoted to him at the Museu d'Art de Catalunya, housed, as at present, in the Palau Nacional de Montjuïc. Picasso also took advantage of the chance to visit the rooms in the museum dedicated to Romanesque art.

The presence of Picasso in Barcelona

Fate brought the young Andalusian artist to a city immersed in a process of modernisation. It was chance more than will which led the Malagan family to put down roots in the heart of a Barcelona which was going through a period of artistic and cultural effervescence. Picasso benefited enormously from this situation, even though he left the city when he was still very young, just 22 years old. The growing fame of the artist after he left Barcelona until the present has helped to permanently link Picasso's name with the history of the city, whilst at the same time contributing to Barcelona's burgeoning international image.

As we have mentioned, after Picasso left Barcelona for good, his return visits were generally short stop-overs on his way to other places in Catalonia. The brevity of these visits did not, however, prevent Picasso from taking part in activities and exhibitions organised in the Catalan capital, and he continued to co-operate in different initiatives organised here throughout his life. Since 1905, when his name was entered on the list of the Association of Catalan Painters and Sculptures, right up to the present, Picasso's presence has been a constant in the artistic and cultural life of Barcelona. Throughout his life, Picasso participated in numerous manifestations, contributed illustrations and, above all, put on exhibitions here. Since his death, his presence in the city has been kept alive by the existence of one of the few monographic museums dedicated to the life and work of the greatest creators of the 20th century, a period which, from the artistic point of view, can be defined as the «Picasso century».

Picasso's ties with Barcelona: family and friends

When Picasso left Barcelona, he left behind him family and friends, bonds which kept him tied forever to the city which had been home to him and which had made him feel, without ever ceasing to be Andalusian, Catalan.

His parents and sister stayed on in Barcelona for the rest of their lives. Lola married Doctor Vilató. The couple had six children, two of them, Fin and Xavier, artists like their uncle.

The devotion of Doña María for her son was important for the conservation of Picasso's early works. This loving mother kept everything the young Pablo had produced up to the moment he left Barcelona. She looked after it carefully and passed on her enthusiasm to her daughter and grandchildren who, after her death, continued to safeguard the enormous legacy left by the artist. The works were kept in the various homes the family lived in until they were finally donated to the city of Barcelona in 1970.

The other tie which linked Picasso with Barcelona forever were the friends he had here. Life-time friends: fellow students at La Llotja Art School, companions in the cultural events at Els Quatre Gats café, studio-mates... and new friends he made during his fleeting return visits to Barcelona or introduced to him by friends at one or other of his French residences. We should mention particularly amongst the friends of the artist various publishers and art gallery owners who promoted publications and exhibitions which helped to keep Picasso's presence alive in the artistic and cultural circles of Barcelona after his departure.

The Museu Picasso de Barcelona

Creation and Development

The existence of the Museu Picasso de Barcelona is the fruit of the artist's relations with the city.

The Museu Picasso first opened its doors to the public on 9 March 1963, after years of negotiations. It started out with an important collection made up of works donated by Jaume Sabartés, Picasso's friend since youth and his personal secretary after 1935, and the Picasso collections from the museums of Barcelona. These collections had been gradually brought together since 1919 when the artist donated his oil painting **Harlequin** at the conclusion of the Art Exhibition organised by Barcelona City Council. The splendid portrait of the ballet dancer Léonide Massine was the first piece in a collection which was gradually built up until the opening of the museum through donations from the artist and other benefactors: gallery owners, publishers, collectors, etc, and through acquisitions. The actual open-

53

ing of the Museum stimulated even more private donations and acquisitions.

Two important events were decisive to the consolidation of the Museum. The first occurred in 1968, when Jaume Sabartés died in Paris. In memory of his friend and secretary, Picasso donated the **Blue Portrait of Jaume Sabartés** (1901) and the entire series of interpretations of Velázquez's **Las Meninas**, comprising 58 oils. The artist also promised to donate a copy of all the engravings he made thereafter, and which he continued to do until his death. Some of these engraved works feature dedications to Sabartés.

The second key event occurred on 23 February 1970, when Picasso signed the donation of the works three generations of his family –his mother, his sister and his nephews and nieces– had jealously guarded. This was a collection of enormous importance made up of 82 oils on canvas, 110 oils on wood, 21 oils on other supports, 681 drawings, pastels and watercolours on paper, 17 albums, 4 books with marginal drawings, an etching and five other objects. Most of these works were produced during the artist's youth, and consolidate the museum as the most important in the world on Picasso's formative years.

The death of the artist, in 1973, did not mean the end of his historic links with the city of Barcelona, quite the contrary, the relation has been kept alive by his family, friends and the Museu Picasso itself.

The bond is further strengthened through the Museum's policy of staging temporary exhibitions, enacted since 1971 and which received renewed impulse in 1982, when such activities were substantially intensified. Two main lines of action were laid down: the first involved exhibitions devoted to Picasso himself featuring works from the Museum or other centres; the second concentrates on shows dedicated to artists or styles in one way or another associated with Picasso. The Museum also promotes seminars and congresses on the theme of Picasso's life and work. All together, these are actions aimed at consolidating the image of the institution all over the world, making the Museum a focal point in the international projection of the city of Barcelona.

Glass and packet of tobacco.

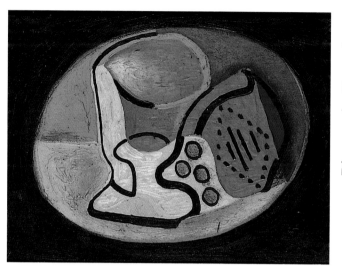

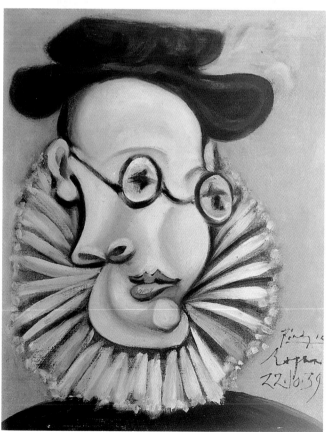

Portrait of Jaume Sabartés with ruff and hat.

Buildings

The Museu Picasso de Barcelona is made up of five buildings, most of them medieval in origin: the Aguilar, Baró de Castellet and Meca palaces, the Casa Mauri and the Palau Finestres, located in Carrer de Montcada. This street begins with the Romanesque Chapel of Marcús (12th century) and ends with one of the architectural jewels of Catalan Gothic, the Cathedral of Santa Maria del Mar (14th century), in the centre of the Ribera district. The museum is situated, then, in an insuperable setting in the heart of the Barcelona where Picasso lived, studied and generally lived life to the full.

Carrer de Montcada, also medieval in origin, is formed, for the most part, by important buildings, palaces and noble mansions built by nobles, merchants and other worthies. Those built in the 13th and 14th centuries are, generally speaking, built around a rectangular courtyard encircled by galleries with an external staircase leading to the first floor, where the master lived. On the ground floor were the services and on the top floor, the servants' quarters.

The buildings forming the museum reflect the harmonisation of the art of various centuries as, in most cases, additions and reforms have been made to the original construction right down to those carried out in the 20th century. Some of these interventions were so important that the building is now known by the name of the person who carried out the reforms and not the original builder, as in the case of the Palau d'Aguilar, which owes its name to the merchant Berenguer d'Aguilar, who bought the palace on 23 November 1463, undertaking large-scale alterations to it. The building still conserves traces of the original 13th-century residence of Jaume Ses Fonts, such as the painted ceilings and the mural decoration. Particularly interesting are the remains of the mural painting depicting the conquest of Majorca by King James I in 1229, now in the Museu Nacional d'Art de Catalunya.

The Palau del Baró de Castellet has a similar history. The palace is documented as far back as the 13th and 14th centuries, but it is nevertheless named after the Baron of Castellet, a title granted by King Charles IV to Marià Alegre d'Aparici i Amat, who was the building's owner and had commissioned the alterations carried out on the building, bought by one of his ancestors, on 16 June 1722. The baron commissioned the construction, in the mid-18th century, of the Neoclassical Room, which features a sumptuous combination of neoclassical and baroque elements. Both palaces were acquired in the 1950s by Barcelona City Council.

The Palau Meca belonged over its history to different lineages, including particularly the family of Ramon Desplà, a knight who was, like his grandfather, councillor-in-chief to Barcelona City Council. In the 16th century, the building was acquired by the Cassador or Caçador family, and passed on to their successors, the marquises of Ciutadilla, first of whom was Josep Meca i Caçador. The building later had various owners until in 1901 the assistance fund Montepío de Santa Madrona established its headquarters here, after which it was absorbed by the foundation of a banking institution which, in turn, reached an agreement with Barcelona City Council in 1977. Much of the original construction has been lost over a history of continuous alteration and reform.

Humorous composition.

In 1981, a project was launched for the reform and extension of the Museu Picasso, completed and inaugurated on 11 January 1982. The work served to connect three palaces, and two more buildings are currently being incorporated, the Casa Mauri and the Palau Finestres. The former is a baroque house dating from the 17th century, with large rectangular porches, balconies with highly moulded projecting stones and thresholds with frieze. The building deteriorated with the passing of time, still conserves a window the wooden lattice, characteristic of 18th-century fronts and which have practically disappeared from Barcelona. For its part, the Palau Finestres conserves traces from the 13th century and the 14th-century front and staircase. The balconies of the first floor and the architraved porches were built in the 16th and 17th centuries.

The collections

The Museu Picasso de Barcelona has some 3,600 works, basically paintings, drawings, engraved work and ceramics.

The painting and drawing section follows chronological order, allowing visitors to follow Picasso's artistic development, from childhood drawings to his last works. To help in the understanding of the works, the works are organised in the different rooms not only chronologically but also thematically, forming an overall vision of the work of the artist in each period of his artistic career.

The Museu Picasso de Barcelona collection begins with a markedly childish drawing of **Hercules**, done in Málaga in November 1890, and with two cut-out figures, a dog and a dove, doubtless dating from the same year. To date, these represent Picasso's artistic beginnings.

Of the formative years, from 1890 to 1899, the Museum has the most complete and important collection in the world. The series of early paintings and drawings are proof of the solid academic training Picasso received thanks to the tutorship given to him by his father and the teachings he received successively from art schools in Corunna, Barcelona and Madrid. At the same time, Picasso also produced a series of works on themes of his own choice. These are scenes of his immediate environment and portraits of the people around him, above all members of his family. These two tendencies, towards the academic and the free, are a constant feature of his work during this formative period.

Picasso's sojourns in Madrid and Horta de Sant Joan, respectively, show him distancing himself from official art and reveal his desire for freedom, facets clearly illustrated in the works he produced in those two places, most of them forming part of the Museum collection.

An important body of works, moreover, illustrate his contacts with the Catalan artistic avant-garde. Particularly interesting are the portraits of his friends which formed part of Picasso's exhibition at Els Quatre Gats in 1900.

Picasso's journeys to Paris from 1900 on allowed him to come into contact with the international avant-garde, and this is reflected in a series of works in a markedly post-Impressionist style using strident colours to depict scenes of squalor and worldliness.

The offering.

The artist's return to the classical canons in 1905, during the Rose Period, is finely illustrated by the **Portrait of Mrs Canals**, a key piece in the museum collections.

The years prior to the Cubism are represented by **The Offering** (1908), which shows the process of rupture in which Picasso was then fully immersed, at a key moment in the evolution of 20th century art, on the threshold of Cubism, the new movement which signified revolution in the world of art.

From the period between the two world wars (1917-1940), the museum's most important works are the series of oils Picasso produced during his stay in Barcelona in 1917. These illustrate the different tendencies in which Picasso was then working: from a late-Cubism, easier to read than his work over the preceding years and in which colour returns to the composition once more: **Blanquita Suarez, Man seated**, etc; a return to classical Mediterranean sources with **Harlequin**; the careful pointillism of **La**

Las Meninas (series).

Salchichona; to the pungent Expressionism of **Horse being gored** which, despite the distance in time, is a clear precursor of **Guernica** (1937).

Amongst the few works from this period conserved in the Museum, particularly outstanding is **Glass and packet of tobacco**, a still life dating to 1924 and carried out at a moment when the artist was extensively experimenting with this genre, one of the most important in his entire artistic career. Also interesting is the **Portrait of Jaume Sabartés with ruff and hat**, the bust of his friend featuring strong deformation and subtle colour schemes which, in spite of all, led Sabartés himself to say: «the fact is that my portrait contains all the features of my physiognomy...»

Las Meninas (series).

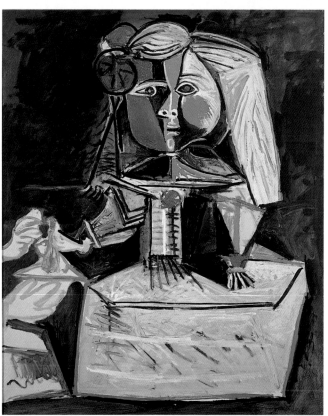

Las Meninas (Infanta Margarita María).

The piano.

In 1957, during a period of interpretative euphoria, Picasso began a series of works based on Velázquez's **Las Meninas**. An intense work of analysis led him to produce 58 oils, 44 interpretations with direct reference to the Sevillian painter, 9 dedicated to the doves in the dovecote in the studio of his house La Californie in the Bay of Cannes, 3 landscapes and 2 free paraphrases. All together, an exhaustive study of composition, rhythm, movement, form and colour in a synthesis of styles created since Cubism. This is the only entire interpretative series in any museum.

Landscape.

Portrait of Jacqueline.

The pigeons.

The pigeons.

The work of Picasso's last years has as its common denominator the search for the very essence of art, and it is therefore no surprise that a subject he was to continual-ly return to throughout his life should emerge forcefully: that of the painter at work in all its variants, such as **Painter at work** (1968) in which certain formal aspects of his so-called late period begin to take shape, the free, sponta-neous stroke, the «shorthand» style, the aesthetic of the *non finito*, etc, all of which are much more strongly evinced in **Seated man** (1969), one of the tarots he presented at the exhibitions in the Palace of the Popes of Avignon in 1970 and 1973.

The museum's collections of engravings and lithographs comprises some 1,500 prints amply demonstrating that Picasso was the greatest engraver of the 20th century as regards number of works, the quality he produced and the creative and technical innovations he introduced to this artistic field. They are also the testimony to the fruitful dia-logue between the engraver and the printer, Picasso work-

The painter at work.

Seated man.

La Minotauromachy.

The Frugal Repast.

Woman with ruff.

65

«La cogida» from
The Tauromachy.

ing with such important printers as Eugène Delâtre, Louis Fort, Roger Lacourière, Aldo and Piero Crommelynck, Mourlot and Arnéra.

The engraving which begins the museum's collection is **The Frugal Repast** (1904), a work which marks Picasso's true beginnings in this field, though he produced his first engraving, **El Zurdo**, in 1899. From those times up to **Suite 156** (on which Picasso worked, basically, between 24 November 1968 and 25 March 1972, and represent his last prints), the Museum has an important collection of engraved work, particularly after 1940. We can mention particularly: **The Minotauromachy** (1935), one of the greatest engravings of the 20th century; the line engraving **Portrait of a Lady, After Cranach the Younger** (1958); the aquatints and a dry-point to illustrate the **Tauromàquia** or **Arte de torear** by José Delgado, alias Pepe Illo, (between 16 March and 5 October 1968); the **347** series and a large number of illustrated books, such as: **Deux contes** (1947) by Ramon Reventós, **Las Meninas et la vie** (1958) by Jaume Sabartés, **El entierro del conde de Orgaz** (1969) by Pablo Picasso...

Ceramic.

The Museu Picasso also has a collection of 41 ceramics donated by Jacqueline Picasso, the artist's last wife, in 1982. These are round, rectangular and oval plates, pots and jugs, most of them made in white or red clay and decorated with slips and copper oxide. Some have incisions, reliefs and engraved motifs, one or two are partially glazed. They form a good example of the technical innovation and rich iconography Picasso employed in his incursions into this most ancestral of the plastic arts.

Home adresses. Studios. Other places

1 Porxos d'en Xifré. Passeig d'Isabel II, 4, baixos.
2 Carrer Cristina, 3, 2º. 2ª
  (on the corner with Llauder).
3 Carrer de la Mercè, 3, 2º.1ª. Building now lost.
4 Carrer de la Plata, 4.
5 La Llotja Art School.
6 Carrer d'Escudellers Blancs.

7 «Els Quatre Gats», Montsió, 3.
8 Riera de Sant Joan, 17. Building now lost.
9 Carrer Nou de la Rambla, 10.
10 Carrer Comerç, 28.
11 Carrer Consulat, 37 (Sabartès' studio).
12 «El Guayaba», Plaça de l'Oli.
   Building now lost.
13 Col·legi d'Arquitectes (Architects'College).
14 Museu Picasso.

Key places in Picasso's Barcelona

Picasso's Barcelona is concentrated in a highly specific part of the city: Ciutat Vella, or old city, and surrounding area.

Near to the Museu Picasso de Barcelona can still be found some of the places where Picasso lived, the schools he studied at, the houses where he installed his studio and the buildings which housed the establishments where he used to go with his friends.

Home addresses:

Passeig d'Isabel II, 4 baixos: Picasso mentioned to his friend Sabartés that on arrival with his family in Barcelona he seemed to recall spending a few days in a small flat rented to them by a friend of his father's on the ground floor of the porticoes known as the Porxos d'en Xifré, built in neoclassical style.

Carrer Cristina, 3, 2on, 2a: Soon after arriving in Barcelona, the family moved to this new address, very close to the first.

Carrer de la Mercè, 3, 2on, 2a: The family moved here in summer 1896. This is in the Mercè barri, or ward, not far from the first two addresses. This new neighbourhood is formed by narrow streets lined by noble palaces and aristocratic mansion. At its heart is the Church of La Mercè, Our Lady of Mercy, patron saint of the city. Picasso's family lived here until 1934, when they moved to Passeig de Gràcia.

Schools:

Escola de Belles Arts de la Llotja: this art school is situated in Carrer del Consolat de Mar and is housed in the old exchange, or Llotja de Comerç, a neoclassical building. Between 1887 and 1901 the director was Antoni Caba. At that time, there was a museum here as well as a school. Many Catalan artists studied here. Picasso attended the school for the 1895-1896 and 1896-1897 academic years.

Cercle Artístic de Barcelona: This «Barcelona Art Circle» is based in the Palau Pignatelli in Carrer dels Arcs. It was created in 1881 to promote the arts. There were rooms here for drawing and painting from real life.

Studios:

The studios of young Barcelona artists at the turn of the century tended to be modest apartments where, as well as working, they would entertain friends and show their works.

Plaça Universitat, 5: Picasso's first studio in Barcelona. In fact, this was the studio of his father's friend, Professor José Garnelo Alda, who was also the brother of Picasso's fellow art student, the sculptor Manuel Garnelo. Picasso came here to work on his large oil, The First Communion.

Carrer de la Plata, 4: Rented for a few days by his father in 1897. Picasso was working on another large oil, Science and Charity, at the time.

Carrer Escudellers Blancs, 1 or 2: near Plaça Reial. Picasso set up his easel here –more a room than a studio, in fact– for a few months in April 1899. The place was sublet to him by his friend and former fellow student, the sculptor Josep Cardona. It was situated on one of the upper floors of a house where Cardona's parents had a workshop for the manufacture of corsets which they sold, according to Richardson, in a shop near their home, at number 3 of the same street, and called «El perfil», which sold a brand of corsets called «La Emperatriz». It was in this room that Picasso met Sabartés. Another frequent visitor to this lively studio was Joan Vidal Ventosa.

Carrer de la Riera de Sant Joan, 17: From January 1900 to the autumn of the same year, Picasso and his friend, the painter Carles Casagemas, shared a studio here which was, according to Sabartés, «on the top floor of an old house in the old part of the city. It is an abandoned place with large windows, of the type known as an "obrador", that is, premises used as an industrial workshop». When Picasso returned to Barcelona after his third visit to Paris, in 1903, he installed his studio here once more, at that time rented by another of his friends, Àngel Fernández de Soto. This street was demolished as part of the work of opening up Via Laietana and integrating it into the urban fabric of the zone.

Carrer Nou de la Rambla, 10: On his return from his second trip to Paris, in January 1902, Picasso shared the studio rented by Àngel Fernández de Soto and where the sculptor Rocarol also worked.

Carrer del Comerç, 28: Picasso installed himself here from January to April 1904, when he left the city for good.

Meeting places:

Els Quatre Gats: at number 3, Carrer de Montsió, housed in the neo-Gothic Casa Martí, which was designed by the architect Puig i Cadafalch. From 12 June 1897 to 26 June 1903, this was the café and meeting-place of the Catalan artistic and cultural avant-garde. Picasso was a regular here, particularly January 1899 and September 1900, though he never stopped going until it finally closed.

Edèn Concert: at 12, Carrer Nou de la Rambla. This was a café and concert hall situated near the Teatre del Liceu. The Catalan writer Josep Pla referred to it as follows: «When the evening performance at El Liceu was over, the important owners of the boxes, in evening dress, gardenia in button-hole, would go, with their lady friends, to have dinner at the Edèn Concert». Josep M. de Sagarra wrote in 1915 that: «(...) the Edèn Concert was the best thing in the old music-hall tradition one could find (...)».

El Guayaba: Plaça de l'Oli, later at 17, Carrer de la Riera de Sant Joan. A studio founded by sculptor, restorer and photographer Vidal Ventosa and Quim Borralleres, a doctor. The name «El Guayaba» is a deformation of the word «Valhalla», the hall where the souls of warriors who died in combat were borne by the Valkyries, according to Scandinavian mythology. The informal group soon became a club with its own premises, firstly situated in Plaça de l'Oli and later transferred to the old studio formerly occupied by Casagemas and Picasso in Carrer de la Riera de Sant Joan, where it remained until the street was pulled down.

Lion d'Or: Plaça del Teatre, 2. Café-Restaurant. One of the most important establishments in the city.

Works by Picasso in Barcelona:

Museu Picasso: in Carrer de Montcada, 15-23 (see chapter on the Museum).

Ceramics Museum (Museu de Ceràmica): Avinguda de la Diagonal, 686. Palau Reial. The collections dedicated to 20th-century ceramics include a series of 16 pieces donated by the artist in 1957.

Catalonia and Balearic Islands College of Architects (Col·legi d'Arquitectes de Catalunya i Balears): Plaça Nova, 5. Friezes on the façade with sgraffiti by the Norwegian artist Carl Nesjar in 1960, based on drawings by Picasso representing popular Catalan themes: one represents Barcelona, the other the sardana, the Catalan national dance.

Biography

– 1881 25 October. Pablo Picasso is born in Málaga, first child of José Ruiz Blasco, painter, teacher at the San Telmo Art School and curator at the City Museum, and María Picasso López

– 1891-1895. The Ruiz Picasso family resides in Corunna.
– 1892 Picasso begins his art studies at the Guarda Art School

– 1895 late September. The family moves to Barcelona
Pablo takes the entrance examination for La Llotja Art School, where he studied for two years

– 1897 October. Begins studies at the San Fernando Art School in Madrid. A frequent visitor to the Prado Museum

– 1898 June. The family returns to Barcelona
Late-June. Moves to Horta de Sant Joan (Terra Alta, Tarragona) invited by his friend Manuel Pallarès

– 1899 January. Returns to Barcelona. Frequents Els Quatre Gats

– 1900 February. First one-man exhibition at Els Quatre Gats
Late-September. First visit to Paris, with Carles Casagemas
Meets Pere Mañach, his first dealer, and first comes into contact with the gallery owner Berthe Weill
Late-December. Returns to Barcelona
New Year's Eve celebration in Málaga with Casagemas

– 1901 28 January. Moves to Madrid
March. Launch of the magazine *Arte Joven*, which he publishes with Francesc d'Assís Soler
25 June-14 July. First exhibition in Paris at the Vollard Gallery, with the Basque painter Iturrino. Meets the poet Max Jacob
Autumn. Beginning of the Blue Period

– 1902 January. Returns to Barcelona
19 October. Leaves for Paris accompanied by Josep Rocarol

– 1903 mid-January. Returns to Barcelona

– 1904 12 April. Fourth and final journey to Paris, accompanied by Sebastià Junyer Vidal. Moves into the building known as the Bateau-Lavoir at 13, Ravignan
Autumn. Meets Fernande Olivier (1881-1966), destined to become his companion until spring 1912

– Early-1905. Beginning of the Rose Period
Early-autumn. Meets Gertrude Stein

– 1906 May. Brief visit to Barcelona
Between 22 and 29 May. Arrives in Gósol (Alt Berguedà. Barcelona)
Mid-August. Returns to Paris.

– Spring 1907. Meets Braque
March-July. Paints **Les demoiselles d'Avignon**
Summer. Meets Daniel-Henri Kahnweiler, his second dealer

– 1908-1914 Braque and Picasso create and develop Cubism
– 1909 early-May. To Barcelona with Fernande
5 June - early-September. Picasso stays in Horta de Sant Joan
– 1910 August. Brief visit to Barcelona, accompanied by Fernande and André Derain and his companion, Alice
– 1911 autumn. Meets Eva Gouel (Marcelle Humbert) (1885-1915)
– 1913 3 June. His father dies. Brief stay in Barcelona for the funeral

– 1916 May. Jean Cocteau introduces him to Serge Diaghilev, director of the *Ballets Russes*. Diaghilev invites him to work on the ballet **Parade**

- 1917 January. Brief stay in Barcelona
  February. Journey to Rome with Cocteau to work with the Ballets Russes
  Meets ballet dancer Olga Kokhlova
  Visits Naples, Pompeii and Florence
  June-November. Visits Barcelona

- 1918 12 July. Pablo marries Olga in Paris

- 1921 4 February. Birth of first child, Paulo

- 1925-1938 Picasso does not participate directly in the Surrealist movement, but his friendship with the writers of the moment often involves him in the group's manifestations
- 1927 January. Meets Marie-Thérèse Walter (1909-1977) with whom he maintains relations until 1936
- 1934 summer. Summer in Spain with Olga and Paulo. Brief visit to Barcelona
- 1935 spring. Breaks with Olga
  5 September. Birth of Maya, fruit of his relationship with Marie-Thérèse Walter
  12 November. Sabartés becomes Picasso's private secretary

- 1936 March-May. Meets Dora Maar (1907-1997), a photographer linked to the Surrealist movement
  18 July. Outbreak of the Spanish Civil War
  20 November. Named honorary director of the Prado Museum in Madrid

- 1937 26 April. Bombardment of Guernica (Basque Country) by German planes
  May-June. Works on the painting **Guernica**

- 1939 13 January. María Picasso López dies in Barcelona

- 1943 May. Meets Françoise Gilot (1921), who will be his companion for ten years

- 1944 5 October. *L'Humanité* announces Picasso's affiliation to the French Communist Party

- 1947 15 May. Birth of Claude, fruit of his relationship with Françoise Gilot
  August. Picasso begins his activity as a ceramist in Vallauris (Provence)

- 1949 19 April. Birth of his daughter Paloma
  Spring. Acquisition of the Fournas studio

- 1953 mid-August. Meets Jacqueline Roque
  Autumn. Separation of Picasso and Françoise

- 1955 11 February. Death of Olga Kokhlova
  Summer. Acquires La Californie, in Cannes, where he lives with Jacqueline

- 1957 August-December. Paints **Las Meninas**

- 1960 27 July. The Museu Picasso de Barcelona is created through an agreement reached by Barcelona City Council

- 1961 2 March. Picasso marries Jacqueline Roque in Vallauris

- 1962 Intense activity as an engraver, work which will continue over the next ten years

- 1963 9 March. The Museu Picasso de Barcelona opens its doors to the public

- 1968 13 February. Death of Sabartés. Picasso renders Sabartés homage by donating, amongst other works, the entire **Las Meninas** series to the Museu Picasso de Barcelona

- 1970 January. The artist makes a large donation to the Museu Picasso de Barcelona, comprising the works his family conserved in their Barcelona home

- 1973 8 April. Pablo Picasso dies in Notre-Dame-de-Vie, Mougins
  10 April. Picasso is buried in the garden of Vauvenargues Castle

Basic bibliography

BRASSAÏ: *Conversaciones*. Madrid, Aguilar, 1964. CABANNE, Pierre: *El siglo de Picasso*, Madrid, Ministerio de Cultura, 1982. CIRICI, Alexandre: *Picasso antes de Picasso*. Barcelona, Iberia, Joaquim Gil, 1972. CIRLOT, Juan Eduardo: *Picasso: el nacimiento de un genio*. Barcelona, Gustavo Gili, 1972. DAIX, Pierre: *La vie de peintre de Pablo Picasso*. Paris, Éditions du Seuil, 1977. OCAÑA, M. Teresa (dir): *Picasso. La formació d'un geni*, 1890-1904. Barcelona, Lunwerg Editores, 1997. PALAU i FABRE, Josep: *Picasso a Catalunya*. Barcelona, Polígrafa, 1967. PALAU i FABRE, Josep: *Picasso vivent: 1881-1907*. Barcelona, Polígrafa, 1980. PENROSE, Roland: Picasso. *Su vida y su obra*. Madrid. Cid, 1959. RAFART i PLANAS, M. Claustre: *Museu Picasso. Guia*. Barcelona, Ajuntament de Barcelona, Direcció de Serveis Editorials, 1998. RICHARDSON, John: *Picasso: una biografía*. Vol. I 1981-1906; vol. II 1907-1917. Madrid. Alianza 1995 (vol. I) and 1997 (vol. II). SABARTÉS, Jaime: *Picasso. Retratos y recuerdos*. Madrid, Afrodisio Aguado, 1953. VALLENTIN, Antonina: *Vida de Picasso*. Buenos Aires, Librería Hachette, 1957. ZERVOS, Christian: *Pablo Picasso*. Cahier d'Art, vol. I, 1932 to vol. XXXIII, 1980.

Catalogues:
Catàleg de pintura i dibuix del Museu Picasso. Barcelona, Servei de Publicacions de l'Ajuntament de Barcelona, 1984. *Picasso i Barcelona*. AINAUD DE LASARTE, Joan (dir). Barcelona, Ajuntament de Barcelona, 1981. *Picasso i els 4 Gats*. OCAÑA, M. Teresa (dir). Barcelona, Museu Picasso-Lunwerg Editores, S.A., 1995. *Picasso. Paisatges 1890-1912*. OCAÑA, M. Teresa (dir). Barcelona, Museu Picasso-Lunwerg Editores, S.A. 1994.

Contents